Inspiring Spaces for Young Children

jessica deviney • sandra duncan • sara harris • mary ann rody • lois rosenberry

This book is dedicated to the children and staff of Children's Discovery Center who constantly inspire us to keep our environments blooming.

Inspiring Spaces
for Young Children

jessica deviney

sandra duncan

sara harris

mary ann rody

lois rosenberry

Lewisville, NC

(c) 2010 Jessica DeViney, Sandra Duncan, Mary Ann Rody, Sara Harris, Lois Rosenberry

Published by Gryphon House, Inc.

PO Box 10, Lewisville, NC 27023

800.638.0928 (toll free); 877.638.7576 (fax)

Graphic Designers: Jessica DeViney, Patrick DeViney

Visit us on the web at www.gryphonhouse.com

Reprinted April 2016

Library of Congress Cataloging-in-Publication Data

Inspiring spaces for young children / by Jessica DeViney ... [et al.].
p. cm.
Includes bibliographical references and index.
ISBN 978-0-87659-317-2
1. Early childhood education--Environmental aspects. 2. Classroom environment. 3. Motivation in education. I. DeViney, Jessica.
LB1139.23.I57 2010
372.16'21--dc22
                    2010003692

Bulk purchase

Gryphon House books are available for special premiums and sales promotions as well as for fund-raising use. Special editions or book excerpts also can be created to specification. For details, contact the Director of Marketing at Gryphon House.

Disclaimer

Gryphon House, Inc. and the authors cannot be held responsible for damage, mishap, or injury incurred during the use of or because of activities in this book. Appropriate and reasonable caution and adult supervision of children involved in activities and corresponding to the age and capability of each child involved is recommended at all times. Do not leave children unattended at any time. Observe safety and caution at all times.

There is no better time than now to start growing a beautiful environment for children. Plant the seed,

Part 2 learning

Part 3 designing

table
of
contents

We value space because of its power to organize ... and its potential for sparking all kinds of social, affective, and cognitive learning.

-Loris Malaguzzi

The warm glow of the sun embraces you as you enter this space. You immediately feel welcome here. Comforts of home surround you—cozy areas for cuddling up with a good book, vibrant plants on the windowsills, a "dining area" with a linen tablecloth and a vase of delicate flowers, family photos respectfully framed, and unique artwork exhibited on shelves around the room. The crystal sun catcher dancing from the ceiling catches your eye. Its reflective light is both calming and invigorating.

As you step further into the room, you are filled with wonder. Vibrant paintings provide a splash of color against the natural canvas of eggshell walls. Outside the window, you are captivated by the beauty of the rose reaching towards the majestic blue sky. Treasures and adventures seem to be hiding around every corner—intriguing items to explore, magical moments to experience, and dreams to discover.

Can you picture this place? Where would such a wondrous place exist? For whom would such a special place be designed? What would be the effects of spending time in such an inspiring environment?

This is an early childhood classroom, probably unlike most classrooms you have seen. In this classroom, relationships are fostered, families are respected, and children are honored. In this classroom, nature's gifts are valued and children's thoughts are captured. In this classroom, learning is alive and aesthetic beauty is appreciated.

Growing an environment that is inspiring and magical for young children is much like growing a seed into a beautiful flower. You have to prepare the soil, make a plan for the garden design, shop for the seeds, plant and water them, and patiently watch them grow from sprouts…to buds…and ultimately to blooming plants.

Creating an aesthetically pleasing environment requires thoughtful planning and the support of your learning community. You cannot achieve this type of environment by adding extra decorations and commercial displays to your classroom. Beautiful classrooms encompass so much more than simply including "beautiful things" in the room. Rather, you must consider the function and adaptability of the space and the dynamic needs and interests of those who inhabit the space.

So where should you begin to create an inspiring classroom? Look around you. Use what you already have in new ways. Keep an open mind. Think outside the box. Close the catalog. Color outside the lines. Find your inspiration. Interview the children about their hopes and dreams. View the world through a child's eyes. Create your inspiring space!

Part

1

inspiring

*No one was ever great
without some portion of divine inspiration.*

-Marcus Tullius Cicero

finding inspiration

To begin to understand the principles of designing beautiful classroom spaces, you must learn to search for what inspires and excites you. Your inspiration may come from a visit to a nearby paint store. Looking at paint chips and browsing the brochures that show how colors work together might spark an idea for a new look for your classroom. Or, the color scheme of a beautifully embroidered pillow that you bought for fifty cents at a yard sale may be your inspiration. Try looking beyond the early childhood catalog and flip through some home decorating catalogs. Consider thinking outside the primary color box. Visit a home store or go to an art gallery. Spend a sunny day at the local nursery or lumberyard. Walk through a resale shop. Borrow your inspiration from anywhere…a fabric remnant, framed children's or commercial art, an authentic piece of furniture, or the beautiful textures and colors of the natural world.

keep reading, because this book will walk you through the process of designing inspiring spaces for young children. The trick is to start small and apply the Seven Principles of Design that are explained and illustrated throughout this book. In addition, you can use the *Rating Observation Scale for Inspiring Environments* (ROSIE), which is the companion observation guide created especially for early childhood professionals.

Finding inspiration is as simple as adopting a new mind-set and looking at the world around you in a new way. Your trip to a community art festival may, at first, seem to focus on looking for a new painting for your living room. But keep an open mind and consider how you might use something that strikes your fancy in your classroom. For example, we found a wooden garden gate at the Scottsdale Art Festival that became our inspiration for displaying children's bird sculptures, and a visit to the Ann Arbor Art Fair inspired us to offer the children in our classroom an experience that integrated tiles, textures, and colors.

This book gives you ideas and projects that you can accomplish in a few minutes, a few hours, or on a weekend. Although there are some ideas that are moderately priced, most of the inspirations cost just a few dollars.

Art Fair Booth Inspiration

An art fair booth sparked inspiration for what became a child-created masterpiece. The children used 1X4 wood planks as small canvases for their artwork.

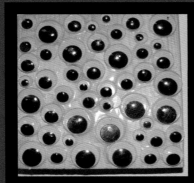

Your excitement and energy intensifies when you walk into places of inspiration. For example, a visit to a local flower shop might inspire an interactive area for little florists. Infinite learning opportunities emerge when children create bouquets, become shoppers, take orders, and calculate purchases.

Home Decorating Store

A shopping excursion to a home decorating store can inspire many ideas for your environment. Seeing shutters in the home decorating store provided the inspiration for using shutters as classroom dividers. You might hang six inexpensive window shutters together with hooks to separate an area of the room. For safety, this divider has been anchored to the floor and ceiling.

Window shutters purchased from a home improvement store provide a cozy backdrop to the home-living area.

finding places for inspiration

Home
Furniture Stores
Carpet, Rug & Tile Stores
Paint Stores
Fabric Shops
Farmer's Markets
Home Improvement Stores
Restaurants & Hotels
Lighting Stores

Media
Internet
Books
TV Makeover Shows
Catalogs & Magazines

Outdoor
Ocean, Lakes, Ponds & Rivers
Forest, Woods & Parks
Outdoor & Pool Showrooms
Nurseries & Landscape Companies
Garden Shops
Sporting Goods Stores
Botanical Gardens

Art
Museums & Galleries
Art & Craft Shows
Hobby Stores
Art Festivals

Resale
Flea Markets
Yard Sales
Auctions
Consignment Shops
Estate Sales

Architectural
Bridges
Windows & Doors
Arches & Columns
Blueprints
Decorative Metal
Fences & Gates

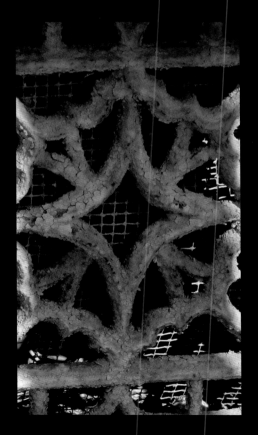

To succeed you need to find something to hold on to, something to motivate you, something to inspire you.

-Tony Dorsett

Inspiring Spaces for Y

Children are miracles. . . we must make it our job to create, with reverence and gratitude, a space that is worthy of a miracle.

-Anita Rui Olds

My first experience with gardening began when I was in first grade with a few flower seeds and a paper cup. After planting the seeds in the moist dirt, all my classmates lined their cups on the sunny ledge near the window. Every morning, Mrs. McCorkle would remind us to water and closely observe our plants. Afterwards, she would write our comments on the big chalkboard in the front of the classroom.

For the longest time, nothing happened in my cup—but I faithfully watered and checked the cup, wondering if it would ever grow. Eventually, up popped some green. A few weeks later, I excitedly gave the flower to my mom for Mother's Day. I do not remember how tall the plant grew….or if it even grew at all, but I do remember Mrs. McCorkle's lesson that you need dirt, water, and sun to grow things. And, I remember that the flower did not pop through the soil overnight—it took time and I needed patience.

-Sandra, Toddler Teacher

Growing Inspiring Spaces—

Three Stages of Growth:

Creating aesthetically inspiring environments for young children happens in three stages—Sprouting, Budding, and Blooming. *Inspiring Spaces for Young Children* and its companion observation guide (ROSIE) lead you through these three stages and show you how to ultimately transform your classroom spaces into islands of beauty. The ROSIE is available through Gryphon House, Inc. For more information on the ROSIE, visit gryphonhouse.com.

SPROUTING

In the SPROUTING STAGE, the plant begins to peek through the dirt and shoots appear. During this stage, you are beginning to understand the principles of designing aesthetically beautiful spaces. Although your environment has started the growing process, time and nourishment are needed to develop into flower buds.

BUDDING

In the BUDDING STAGE of growth, you are becoming more competent in creating inspiring spaces. As your knowledge increases about design principles and aesthetic components, your environment continues to develop into a cluster of buds.

BLOOMING

The BLOOMING STAGE is the period of time when the plant is at its highest level of growth and it glows with health and beauty. It is during this stage that you have reached your fullest potential in designing beautiful and inspiring spaces for children and adults.

SPROUTING   **BUDDING**   **BLOOMING**

Inspiring Spaces for Young Children is for everyone. Perhaps your environment needs some initial watering, sunlight, and nourishment. Or, maybe you are looking for some new growth. Producing fruit, reaching the peak of health, and creating a glow are the goals of the blooming stage. It is at this final stage that your classroom is alive and beautiful and a place where children and adults grow and reach their fullest potential.

Tips

- Be patient. Growth takes time.
- Start small. Focus on one improvement at a time.
- Change what you can. Know that some ideas may be outside your ability to take on.

Take a close look at your classroom. What is your environment's stage of growth? Do you see a Sprouting, Budding, or Blooming environment? Whether your space is only in its seedling or sprouting state—with the nutrients stored and ready to grow—or your classroom has already started sprouting and budding, the fact that your space exists means there is a seed there ready to grow.

So, keep reading and transform your classroom environment into an inspiring and beautiful space. Examining children's spaces through aesthetic lenses will inspire you to create an environment that goes beyond the traditional high standards of the quality rating scales and the esteemed accreditation status. *Inspiring Spaces for Young Children* encourages you to create spaces that are not only carefully and intentionally designed, but also are places of beauty that support learning, stimulate imaginations, nurture children, families, and staff—and truly inspire the wonderful memories of childhood.

Even the wildest dreams have to start somewhere. Allow yourself the time and space to let your mind wander and your imagination fly.

-Oprah Winfrey

Part

2

learning

Just living is not enough...one must have sunshine, freedom, and a little flower.

-Hans Christian Anderson

seven
principles
of design

principle 1

nature inpires beauty

principle 2

color generates interest

principle 3

furnishings define space

By infusing elements of key design principles, you can create a classroom that intrigues, invites, and stimulates many senses. The design principles ,when layered together, heighten the overall feeling of the room. Sparking the interest of a child cannot be done by simply placing furniture in an empty room. The space must be formed with all seven principles to be seen in full bloom.

principle 4

texture adds depth

principle 5

displays enhance environment

principle 6

elements heighten ambiance

principle 7

focal points attract attention

When they are implemented, these design principles will motivate all who enter your space, stimulate those that occupy your space, and enliven those whose interest in the space is beginning to fade.

defining the principles

Inspiring Spaces for Young Children and ROSIE offer Seven Principles of Design that help make the trip down your garden path smooth and beautiful.

principle 1:   nature inspires beauty

Just as you are immersed in a natural world of sights, sounds, tastes, smells, and textures, classrooms should reflect the wonders of nature that surround you. As children interact with nature, they deepen their understanding and appreciation of their places and roles as caretakers of the planet.

principle 2:   color generates interest

Color can be a powerful design principle both in positive and negative ways. Proper use of color can create a mood, define a space, and reflect children's homes and communities. Used negatively, color can be overpowering, confusing, and over-stimulating.   A neutral background for your classroom with a few well-chosen accent colors will create interest that is focused on the children and adults who inhabit the space.

principle 3:   furnishings define space

Furnishings are used to identify classroom areas such as dramatic play, blocks, art, music, and science. When these furnishings are authentic and sized and placed properly, children's play will increase in quality and depth.

principle 4:   texture adds depth

Texture in the environment offers visual interest and depth and provides children with unique tactile experiences. As children interact with sensory elements, they sharpen their observational skills and fine motor abilities through the languages of weaving, sculptures, and textiles.

principle 5:   displays enhance environment

By eliminating clutter, arranging storage materials, and highlighting children's work, the classroom becomes a backdrop to honor all who occupy the space.

principle 6:   elements heighten ambiance

Multiple sources of light create an ambiance of relaxation and contemplation. By using light in supportive ways, children are able to interact creatively with others and the environment.

principle 7:   focal points attract attention

When entering the classroom, a distinct focal point can highlight interactive learning centers, children's work, an architectural element, or a beautiful artifact. Focal points invite children to actively engage and participate in the environment.

Design can be art.

Design can be aesthetics.

Design is so simple,

 that is why it is so complicated.

-Paul Rand

principle **1** : nature inspires beauty

Nature champions a beautiful perspective of the world.

-Sandra Duncan

A tree branch, painted red, hangs from the ceiling and creates visual interest.

Living items such as plants, animals, and rocks spark curiosity about nature.

Ocean scenes created with recycled blue materials provide opportunities for imaginative play.

Faux wood vinyl flooring defines the area and provides a protective surface.

bringing
the
outside in

Whether you live in the desert or mountains, city or countryside, warm or cold climate—the beauty of nature is universal.

Incorporating natural elements inside the four walls of your classroom can effortlessly transport children into a world of beauty. Not only does nature provide an infinite supply of sensory experiences that can be integrated into all learning domains, it conveys a sense of calmness and tranquility for both children and adults.

Bringing elements of the natural world into your classroom is easy and affordable, and children will enjoy its essence and artfulness.

Tree trunk cross sections display natural elements and children's nature-inspired art.

(insect impression in clay)

infusing nature into classrooms

Classrooms should be filled with natural or living elements such as plants, rocks, herbs, seashells, twigs, small animals, fresh flowers, and fish. Not only are natural items great learning tools, but they also enhance your space with beauty. There are many simple and imaginative ways to bring the outside into your classroom.

Adding children's clay sculptures to a birdhouse connects children to the space.

Wind chimes make musical sounds as children move throughout the room.

Natural materials offer unique opportunities for sorting and investigating.

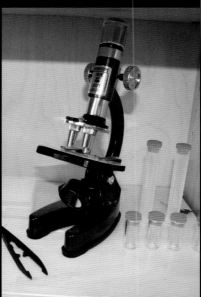

Scientific items invite children to test theories with natural elements.

Window

Natural elements hung from a tension rod and fishing line catch the sunlight as it shines through.

Floor

The floor holds natural objects such as plants, large wicker baskets, tree stumps, or sea grass rugs.

Incorporate natural elements on multiple surfaces to immerse children in nature.

Nature provides a blank canvas of open-ended opportunities to think, create, and investigate.

from *Reggio Children*

Ceiling Suspended birch branches guide children visually into the area and create spaces to hang children's work or found natural elements.

Wall A folding leaf screen provides aesthetic appeal and inspiration for children's weaving.

Table Tables give children space to investigate, examine, and manipulate natural materials.

experiencing nature with the senses

TACTILE

Experience nature through touch

Sift sand and pebbles

Identify natural elements through touch

Walk barefoot over a natural texture path

Sand wood smooth

VISUAL

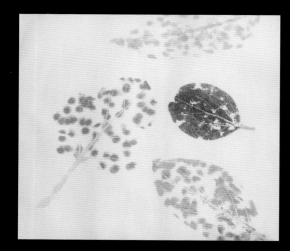

Transfer leaf's pigment with a hammer

Make nature imprints in clay

Paint with dye made from blueberries

Create rubbings from bark

Weave with grass and stems

OLFACTORY

Infuse scents through aromatic plants

Arrange fresh flowers

Match food scents with flavors

Peel and smell oranges or lemons

Build with pine branches

COGNITIVE

Sort elements on a lazy Susan

Place tree twigs by width or length

Categorize seashells by shape or color

Count tree rings to determine age

Write with tree twigs in sand

AUDITORY

Listen to water trickle over a rock fountain

Make sounds by pouring water

Hear ocean sounds in conch shells

Listen to nature soundtracks

Crunch dried leaves

Nature champions a beautiful perspective of the world. Through interacting and experiencing natural elements, children learn by seeing, touching, smelling, hearing, and sometimes tasting. Integrating nature into the classroom not only promotes learning but creates a beautiful environment.

Mysterious Sprouting

During a nature project, a teacher planted seeds in the sensory table without the children knowing. The teacher wanted to see their reactions once the seedlings appeared in a place used for scooping, pouring, and measuring sand. It took over a week before something started to grow. Josi, who was responsible for watering the plants in the science center, was first to notice. "Look! Look! Something is growing in that table!" The children started to speculate about how the bean sprouts got into the table. "It's magic!," said Tyler. "No it's not!," countered another child. After much deliberation, they came to the conclusion that someone put the bean sprouts there. This experiment provided an opportunity for the children to hypothesize about where seeds could grow. The children then tried planting seeds in different types of soil and predicting which soil was the best for growing plants. And, best of all, the sprouts brought nature's beauty to the environment.

Be sure to have a bounty of natural elements available for children to discover.

Meadow

flower petals, pressed
fern, pumpkins, corn
husks, dried corn, lentils,
wheat, grasses, oats,
plants, cattails, gourds

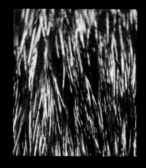

Textiles

bristle brushes, leather,
fur, raw cotton

Water

driftwood, seashells,
sea fans, coral, sea glass,
cattails, sandstone, river
rock, sea sponges, sand,
seaweed, tabletop water
fountains

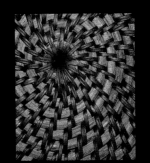

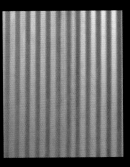

Minerals

gemstones, granite,
fossils, marble,
sandstone

Items made from natural materials

cork tiles, barn siding,
rice paper, pottery,
glass beads, parchment
paper, stone tiles, pasta,
potpourri, wood floors
or doors, sea grass rugs,
cloths (silk, cotton, wool),
wicker baskets, twine

Metals

steel, brass,
aluminum, copper

Woods

tree branches & twigs,
pine cones, pine
needles, nuts, magnolia
pods, coconuts, leaves,
bamboo, tree stumps,
eucalyptus, pussy
willows, tree bark, tree
"cookies" (slices of tree
trunk), dried berries &
herbs, petrified wood,
moss, ferns, fossils

Nature has been for me, for as long as I remember, a source of solace, inspiration, adventure, and delight; a home, a teacher, a companion.

-Lorraine Anderson

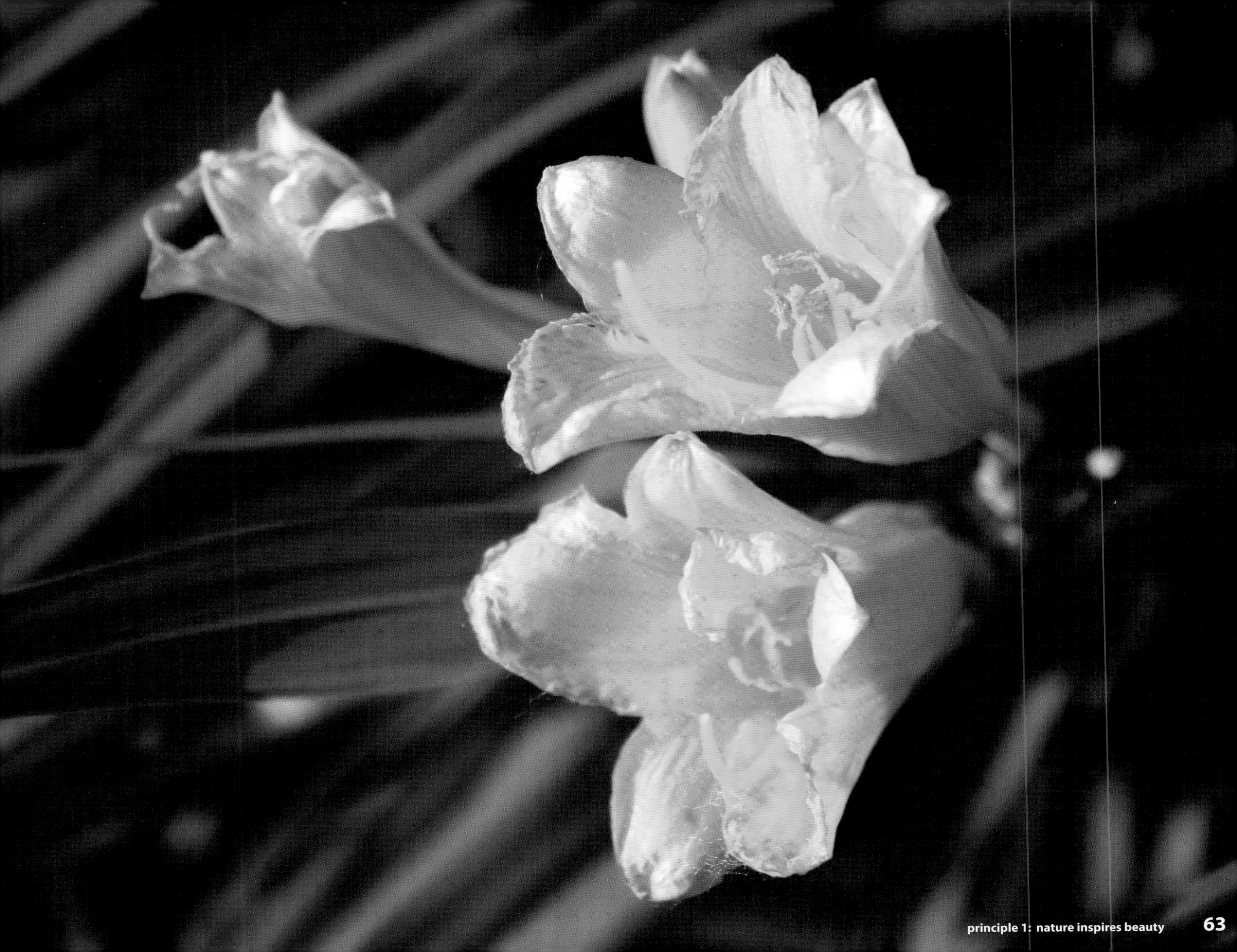

principle **2**: color generates interest

I used to tape colored shapes on the tables to identify work and eating areas. Now, I hang clear acrylic ornaments filled with various colors and textures above the tables. The children enjoy changing the contents and discussing what's inside.

-Andrea, Preschool Teacher

Color can be powerful in both positive and negative ways. It can evoke feelings and emotions, give importance to areas or objects, define spaces, and reflect children's homes or communities. Sometimes, however, color can have a negative effect. Using many colors in a classroom results in a chaotic feeling because it is too visually stimulating. Also, keep in mind the intensity of the colors in the classroom. Bright yellows, reds, and blues can overwhelm children's emotional well-being, so use primary colors conservatively.

When you look at your classroom walls, how many items do you see hanging around the classroom? Other than the children's work, how many different colors do you see? Are they mostly primary colors? If your walls look like most preschool classrooms, you likely counted a pretty high number…and the majority of colors you observed were bright and primary colors. Consider this: If you cannot see at least 75% of the walls and the majority you see (other than children's work) are brightly colored, you may have visual clutter. The impact of this visual clutter results in reducing or eliminating the open white spaces necessary to let your eyes and mind relax. The space becomes visually chaotic. By significantly reducing the bright colors and pattern clutter, you create a visually tranquil environment for young children.

Classroom with a neutral color palette

Classroom using multiple bright colors

Take a look at the clothes in your closet. Which clothes are your reliable standbys? Did you choose a white shirt, pair of khaki pants, or black skirt? These "go to" items may be your favorites because they are neutral colors. You can pair them with the latest and trendiest color of the season and they are instantly modernized. Just as your neutral-colored pants can be updated with the latest colored shirt, a neutral colored classroom can be modernized with splashes of trendy colors.

Most centers do not have an abundance of money to spend on paint, wall coverings, and carpets. Therefore, when choosing colors for larger items, it is important to think neutral as these colors tend to outlast trends. Then, bring in splashes of trendy colors with inexpensive decorative elements such as area rugs, wall hangings, pillows, and children's artwork. Replace these decorative items when a new color trend appears.

following the color wheel

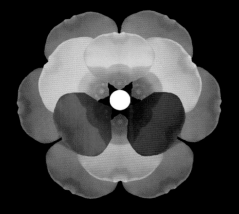

Primary

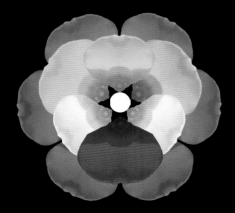

Complementary

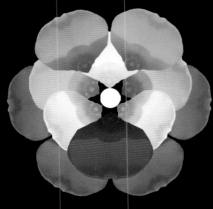

Split Complementary

Tips for choosing colors

- Choose colors that are complementary or split complementary on the color wheel to guarantee an aesthetically pleasing palette for your environment.
- Use websites that offer the latest information on color trends.
- Incorporate current color trends by reading decorating magazines or visiting a home decorating or paint store.

Paint

Inspiration for paint color can come from visiting home decorating or improvement stores where you can find current color trends from paint chips or from sales associates. Many popular paint brands also have websites you can visit to learn about the latest color trends.

Fashion

Clothing and accessories offer insight into the latest color trends. Inspirations for your environment come from observing how colors are combined in fashion.

discovering color inspirations

Artwork

Inspiring color schemes emerge when you reflect the color palette of a child's masterpiece or purchased artwork.

Nature

Nature never goes out of style so take color cues from surrounding landscapes. Observing a flower saturated with orange and yellow might inspire you to inject those colors into your own space.

Furnishings

Classroom furnishings that mirror current color trends can provide inspirational color schemes. To determine if your classroom furnishings reflect current color trends, compare them with colors seen in home decorating stores, shows, websites, and catalogs.

Restaurants

Because they are designed by commercial interior designers, bistros, cafes, and upscale hotel restaurants are terrific places to observe trendy combinations of colors used on walls, flooring, and table settings.

choosing accent colors

The purpose of accent colors is to draw your attention to a particular object or special area. Be intentional about where you place accent colors in the classroom. Use an accent color to attract children to a specific area.

Authentic items such as red shutters and chair bring this space to life by adding a realistic place for play and a pop of color.

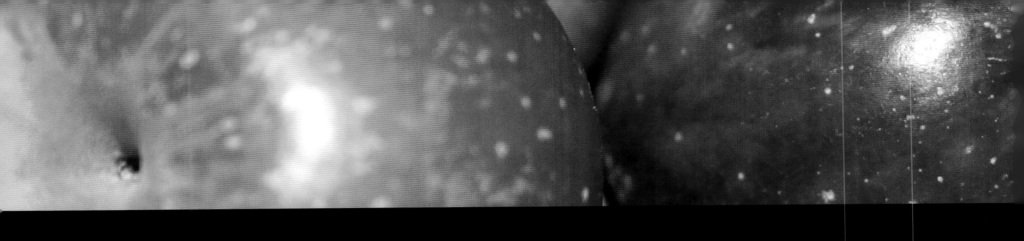

aturating your entire classroom with bold colors is visually over-stimulating, but accent colors generate interest.

Accent colors can be integrated into fabric panels, pictures, rugs, wall coverings, furniture, and authentic items.

using accent colors

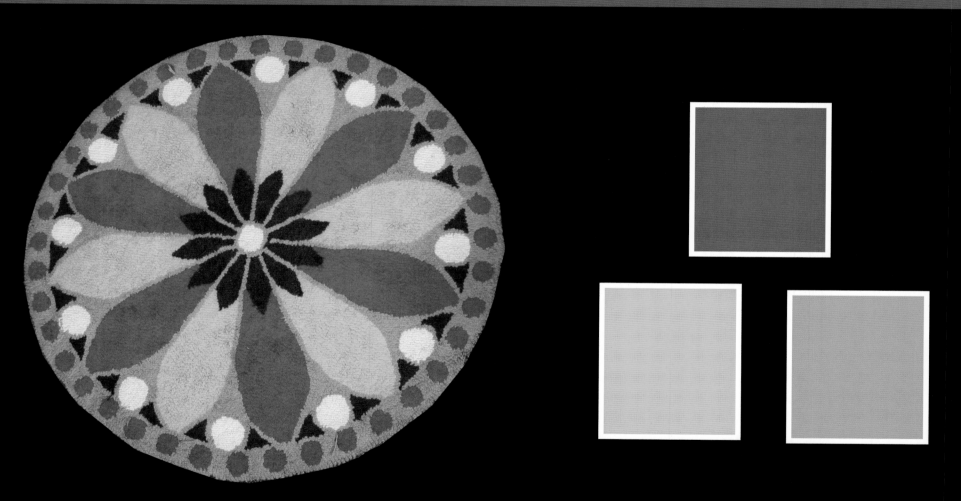

Gather color-coordinating elements.

Incorporate it into your space.

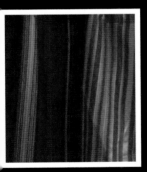

defining spaces with color

Accentuating a classroom area through the use of color helps define the space. It is important, however, not to use too much color. Bring balance to the room by using no more than three coordinating colors.

Questions to ask when choosing colors

- What colors should be added to generate interest?
- Are there areas in the classroom that need camouflaging?
- What architectural elements could be accentuated with color?
- Is there enough white space to bring attention to the colors?

creating interest

Tip
Use large painted or fabric-covered canvases that can be changed with ease when children's interests or color trends change.

Color sets the stage for provoking children's interests through paint, textiles, furniture, and accessories. Because color is such a powerful element in creating interest, be sure to use it carefully.

Color can enhance architectural elements. Using a shade or tone slightly different from the overall wall color creates drama and draws attention.

Color can camouflage an undesirable architectural element. For example, this uninteresting pillar has been transformed into a beautiful white "birch tree."

Nature's powerful colors enrich the world .

-Anonymous

principle3 : furnishings define space

Space has to be a sort of aquarium that mirrors the ideas, values, attitudes, and culture of the people who live within it.

-Loris Malaguzzi

defining and maximizing spaces

Inhabiting a classroom is much like living in an urban loft. Typically, a loft is an open space that serves multiple functions. Areas may be arranged by sectioning off the bedroom with a privacy screen, defining a living space with a sofa, or placing a rug in the dining area. The same is true for designing a classroom. Although you have many different areas—for example, blocks, home-living, and science—in one small space, it is important to consider the entire room when choosing and placing furnishings.

A curved bamboo wall creates a unique way to define this space and provide transparency.

The cityscape pictures represent real-life transportation and construction, and they help define the space.

SCIENCE

Like an urban loft, the vast majority of preschool classrooms do not occupy a large amount of square footage. Although there are a few things you can do to make your classroom space appear larger, the bottom line is there may not be many square feet available. Consequently, it is important that everything in your classroom has a purpose, contributes to children's learning, and is aesthetically pleasing.

When floor space is limited, consider using the wall for a learning center.

estions to ask when space mited

What piece of furniture can be used in multiple ways?
Can a learning center also be used for group meetings?
What can be discarded because it does not enhance children's learning?
Can walls be used to create an area?

Tips

- Another versatile piece of furniture is an ottoman, which can be used for storing books and as a place to sit.

An armoire is a versatile piece of furniture that can be placed in multiple learning centers and used in various ways. Make it a place for display or storage. Leave the cabinet doors open to invite children to interact with the treasures inside.

creating
a cozy retreat

Children need time for quiet reflection, just as adults do, and so it is important to have a designated space where they can be alone. Partitioned away from the classroom's main traffic area, this space should be designed as a cozy retreat. Elements such as pillows, upholstered chairs, and rugs add softness. Lighting enhances the ambiance.

This cozy retreat is tucked away under a loft. The fireplace was made using extra siding mounted onto plywood. A battery operated light, adult chairs without the legs, a rug, fire wood, and coffee table were added to the space to give it an authentic feel.

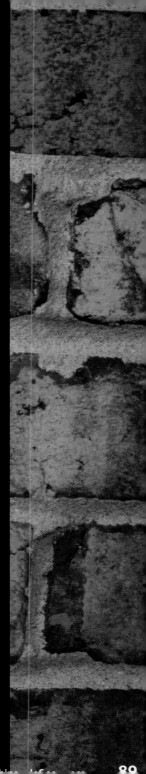

positioning furniture

This home-living center is defined by positioning the furniture and rug at unique angles with the rest of the room.

furnishings
mirror life

Include authentic materials in all areas of the classroom so that the children's play experiences mirror real life. The term "authentic" refers to an object that is commonly seen or used in an adult space but is placed in a child's environment for aesthetic or functional purposes.

A small sink inserted into a plywood frame makes this home-living area feel real.

Ideas for authenticating areas

Small
Authentic Items

- tool belt
- tablecloth/place mat
- telephone
- road map
- street sign
- artist palette
- cutting board
- lantern
- tray
- colander
- oven mitt
- dish towel
- measuring tape

Large
Authentic Furnishings

- coffee table
- armoire
- buffet
- music or plant stand
- adult chair or sofa
- charcoal grill
- fireplace
- trunk
- mannequin
- bench
- rug
- wooden dresser
- pedestal

Home-Living Area

Creating an inspiring home-living area goes beyond traditional housekeeping equipment. Children experience, learn, and test ideas in spaces that reflect everyday encounters. Dramatic play comes to life by adding an authentic piece of furniture. A buffet enriches the home-living area into a restaurant or fancy dining space. An armoire transports the children into grandma's attic. Even store mannequins or racks expand children's knowledge about merchandise and give them an opportunity to role play as a sales associate or customer.

Ideas for authenticating the home-living area

- Set table with items such as silverware, plates, large serving bowls, and cups.
- Dress the dolls.
- Place the dolls as you would in real life with just one doll in the bed or chair.
- Add small authentic items.
- Position large authentic furnishings.
- Incorporate plants and greenery.
- Illuminate space with table, floor, or ceiling lights.

Block Area

Many block areas contain wooden or plastic blocks and store-bought cars or people. Add unique materials to bring new intrigue to the space. Designate an area where children can build with found, recycled, and textured blocks. A rug, wooden platform, and/or a table offers a protected building space.

As children develop diverse scenes, they may desire more items to complete their imaginative play. Add landscaping elements by creating trees out of tubing, wire, and paper. Offer clay so they can sculpt families, pets, and neighborhoods.

Ideas for authenticating the block area

- hard hats
- tool belts
- measuring tapes
- graph paper
- drawing utensils
- blueprints
- photos of buildings
- architectural books
- road signs
- found materials
- loose parts: tubes, hoses, plastic pipes
- cones
- sculptures of buildings
- maps

Questions to ask when enriching the block area

- In what ways can materials be organized by size, type, and function?
- How can different levels or heights be created for children's building and constructing?
- Other than wood or plastic blocks, what unconventional materials can be included?
- What kinds of unique textures can be incorporated?
- How can technology extend learning?
- In what ways can light (i.e., overhead projector, flashlights, glow sticks, rope lights) enhance this space?
- Are there natural materials (i.e., pebbles, tree bark, twigs) available for children to use?

We created a block area filled with many kinds of building blocks, paper, fabric, lights, and recycled materials where children were free to explore. The children built a castle tower, flowing river, and rickety bridge. This opportunity to use new and different materials opened the door for the children to expand the endless possibilities of their imaginations.

-Katie, Kindergarten Teacher

Art Area

Enhancing the art area's many surfaces with authentic and practical items stimulates children to create beautiful masterpieces.

Ideas for authenticating the art area

- artist brushes
- charcoal pencils
- drawing pencils
- gum erasers
- canvases
- sketch pads
- watercolor paper

- paint cups with covers
- easels
- painting smocks
- pastels
- rulers
- ribbon
- assorted found materials

- watercolor/acrylic paints
- paint palettes
- drawing paper
- graph paper
- tissue paper
- clay and tools
- modeling dough

easel

shelf

wall

multiple surfaces

Science
Area

Found, recycled, natural, and mechanical items offer children many opportunities to explore and organize materials. Creating areas to test theories, explore textures, and investigate materials expands children's growth in scientific inquiry.

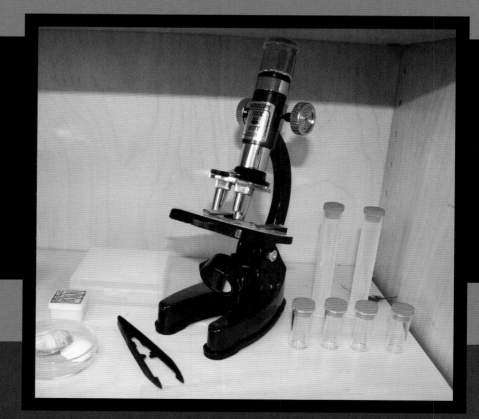

Ideas for authenticating the science area

- magnifying glasses
- magnets
- microscope
- measuring cups
- measuring tape
- balance
- small scale
- plants
- flashlights
- sectioned containers

- live creatures
- various sized containers
- nature items
- authentic books
- notebooks to record and document
- fur
- mirrors
- bird's nest
- test tubes

When displaying numerous items, it is important to keep in mind the visibility of each one. The space loses children's interest when it is overwhelmed with items that are placed without purpose. Add some inexpensive or repurposed items such as blocks or cups to lift up the materials in the back.

Music Area

Extend children's ability to explore music beyond a basket of instruments. Promote visual and auditory learning by openly displaying instruments on walls, floor, and shelves. Fill the space with recorders, keyboards, guitars, CD players, music stands, a conductor's platform, and multicultural instruments.

Ideas for authenticating the music area

- drums
- tambourines
- bells
- scarves
- ribbons
- guitars
- sheet music
- music books
- keyboards
- rain sticks

- music stand
- CD player
- CDs of various cultures and types
- rhythm sticks
- musical triangles
- karaoke machine with microphone
- musical instruments from many cultures

Library Area

Reflect intimacy and warmth in the children's library area with items that might be found in an adult's living room. By incorporating a rug, coffee table, pillows, plants, book rack, and soft lighting, the space feels serene. The layered textures create depth and invite children to come in, get cozy, and enjoy a book.

Ideas for authenticating the library area

- ottoman
- adult chair
- pillow
- rug
- small lamp
- low shelves
- books representing many cultures
- baskets

To make the space more inviting, add authentic pieces such as a gas fireplace and bookshelves. These items are similar in cost to children's furniture but provide a welcome and unexpected twist in an early childhood classroom.

Communication Area

Ideas for authenticating the communication area

- letter stamps
- typewriter
- alphabet
- graph paper
- stencils
- t-square
- rulers
- computer
- printer
- clock
- mailboxes
- ink pad
- drafting table
- receipt book
- notebooks
- adding machine
- head sets
- tape recorder
- letterhead

A communication area encourages children to write, draw, send letters, and develop all-important fine motor skills. Be sure to fill this area with many different types of authentic communication tools, as well as books and photographs.

Inspiring Spaces for Young Children

An environment is a living, changing system. It conditions how we feel, think, and behave; and it dramatically affects the quality of our lives.

-Jim Greenman

principle 4 : texture adds depth

Textures are the visual and tactile spice of life.

-Rusty Keeler

finding textures

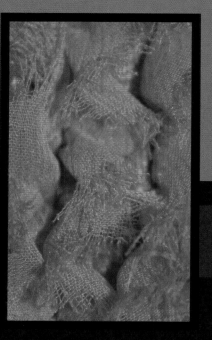

Textures surround us. Soft, hard, bumpy, shiny, rough, and smooth textures are everywhere. Encourage children to explore textures to gain a new understanding of the world around them.

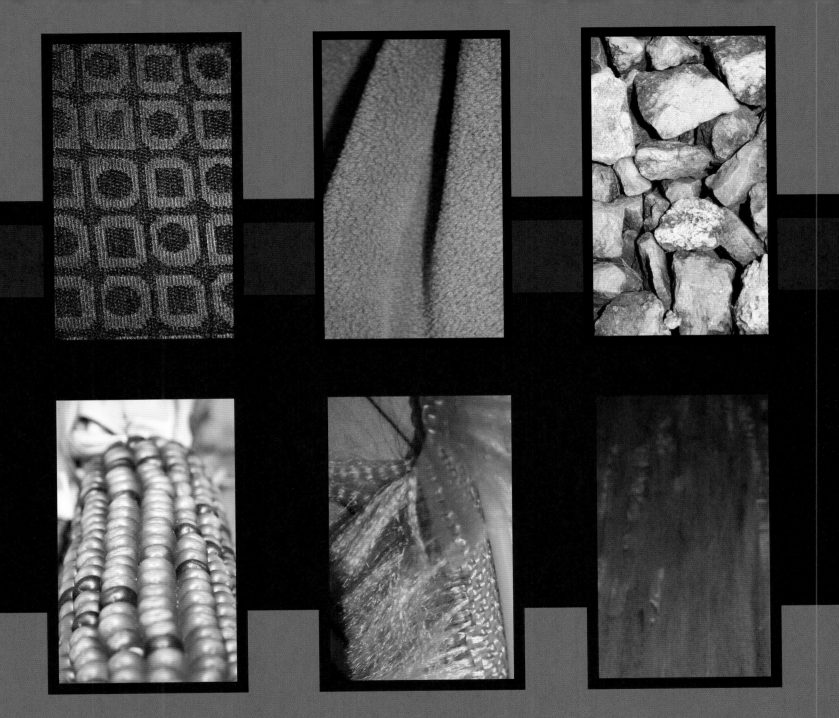

weaving
tactile materials

A twig mobile provides visual interest and honors children's weaving. Look for weaving backdrops that contain holes or slats. Place mats, wall hangings, frames, wheels, colanders, and homemade weaving panels make wonderful weaving canvases.

layering multiple textures

Layering textures on floors, walls, ceilings, and shelves creates a living textural sculpture that fills the room.

Twigs hug the support beam.

Drums are layered on a sisal rug.

A privacy screen is deconstructed.

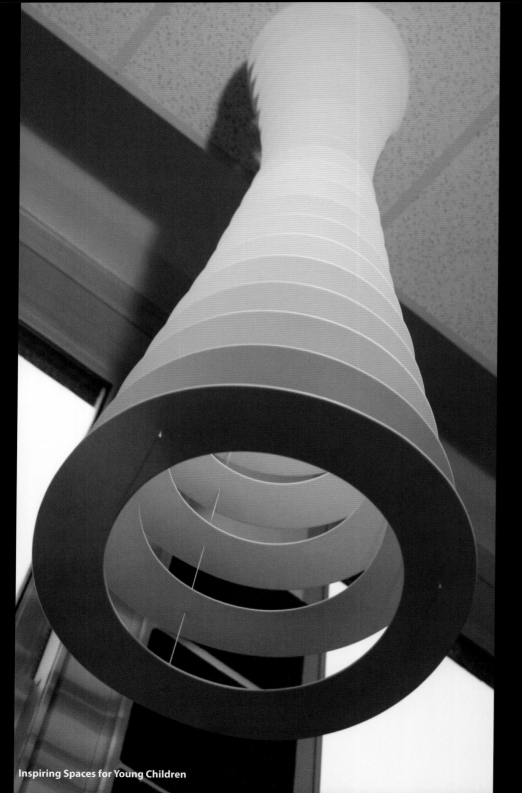

infusing visual textures

Incorporating visual textures into a room brings depth to an ordinary-looking, flat environment. Spaces begin to flourish by adding textured items to the floor, ceiling, and walls.

Children learn about their senses through exposure to various textures. It is easy to add interactive textures to the classroom because they can be found everywhere. Many different kinds of textured scraps at minimal to no cost can be found at recycle stores, sign shops, and plastic manufacturers. So get creative, ask for donations, and boost children's excitement about the beautiful world of texture.

sensory tables

Tips

- If you are concerned about children becoming over-stimulated, try adding one texture at a time to the sensory table.

creating interactive scenes

Sensory tables provide limitless opportunities for play and explorative learning. Dramatic play scenes and stories can be told from children's perspectives by adding materials (including found, recycled, and natural items) and toys or manipulatives (such as plastic vehicles, animals, insects, beads). Allowing children's interest to guide what is needed to create these sensory table scenes empowers them and builds many aspects of their development.

Ideas for enhancing the sensory table

- cups
- funnels
- colored water
- tubes
- bowls

- watering can
- shovels
- sifters
- natural materials
- recycled materials

A tray filled with sand might be uninspiring. However, when children interject their ideas to create scenes or landscapes that interest them, an ordinary thing becomes extraordinary. For example, the children in one class longed for desert views, and so they decided to make their own. Molding clay with toothpicks to sculpt cacti, they began to set the backdrop in which they could create endless desert stories.

*Using texture allows you to add
another whole dimension to a space.*

-Lewitin

principle**5** : displays enhance environment

Children's nature collections breathe life into displays.

-Mary Ann Rody

Nature's beauty fills children with a sense of wonder about their world. Pinecones, for example, may seem ordinary to adults but create amazement in children's eyes. A walk in the neighborhood park to collect treasures such as pinecones, twigs, bark, wild flowers, and leaves stimulates children's imaginations. After gathering items that they find interesting, they make decisions about displaying their collections.

awakening spaces with children's collections

Questions to consider when displaying children's collections

- What makes the collection items special?
- Which collection items should be displayed?
- Where should the collection items be displayed?

investigating

After collecting nature items from the local park, children investigate their collections. Children sort by attributes, uniqueness, and personal preferences to decide which are special to them.

Tips for sorting found materials

- Designate a space with baskets, buckets, and clear containers.
- Provide a wooden table with dividers.
- Use a shelf with bins that can easily be removed for sorting on the floor.
- Offer outdoor window boxes or containers placed near classroom door.

When children investigate found materials, they learn about nature and create a bond with the world around them. Children develop a sense of ownership toward their collections and may choose to offer their found gifts to the classroom.

selecting

After sorting their collected items, children discuss and select which treasures to gift to the classroom. Allowing children to collaborate in the selection and decision-making process fosters group consensus and shared meaning. More importantly, it gives the children pride and ownership of their classroom displays.

An acrylic tray and bowls provide space for sorting.

"Exploring the
Natural World
Around Us"

displaying

Children can think creatively about how and where to display their treasures in unique ways when you offer many surfaces such as walls, floors, windows, and shelves.

A natural twine banner purchased at a craft store and draped across windows provides an area for children to insert and display the items they collect.

Children need a place that is personalized and meaningful. Therefore, it is important to incorporate elements of their culture, artwork, and interests to give them a sense of belonging and build a symbolic relationship between themselves and the spaces they occupy.

personalizing spaces through displays

After completing the masks, children gave them to the classroom as gifts.

Questions to consider when personalizing space

- How can children personalize space with gifts?
- How can displays represent real life?
- How can displays reflect the value of children's work?

children's gifts personalize the space

Intrigued by our school's surroundings, the children went on a walk in our community and discovered the riverfront. They took photographs of the harbor, fishermen, docks, boats, and bridge. The pictures the children gifted to our school reflect their perspectives. We chose salvaged window frames to display their photographs, giving them even more importance.

-Jen, Preschool Teacher

Children need opportunities to personalize their classroom with drawings, photographs, paintings, sculptures, child-crafted manipulatives, and found materials.

displays represent real life

Fresh flowers inspire a child's masterpiece.

Clay sculptures are inspired by fresh apples.

displays represent real life

Children used pens and tempera paint to express the metamorphosis of a butterfly.

The beauty of the sun is represented through children's weaving.

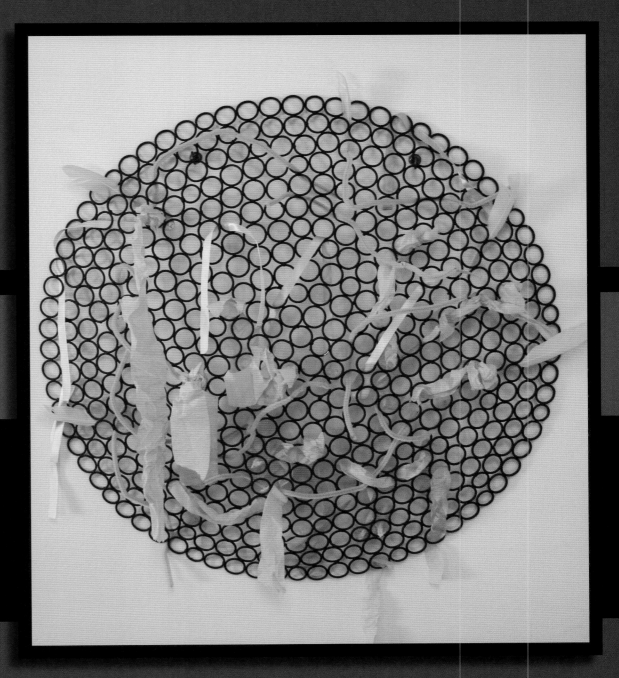

A seemingly insignificant item is dignified by placing it in an area of importance. Walls and ceilings present unique opportunities to highlight children's work.

displays reflect value

Children's sculptures, placed on the heightened surface of a candlestick holder or wooden platform, are more visible and given a sense of worth.

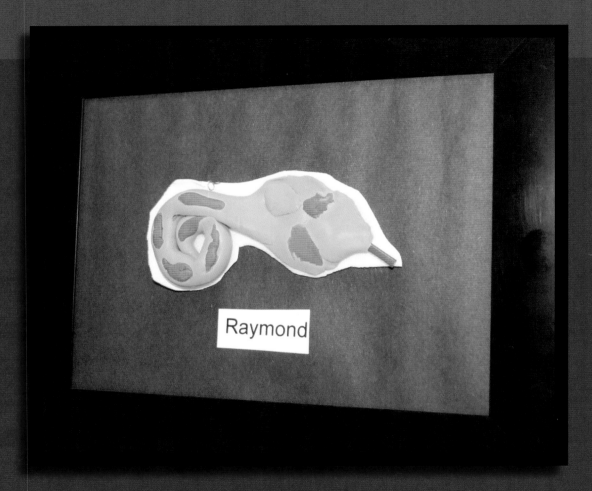

Framing children's artwork communicates the importance of their work. Just as an expensive piece of art is framed, children's framed work signifies that it is an equally important element in the room.

Framing can be accomplished in many different ways such as matte board, black construction paper, poster board, covered box lids, and wooden or metal frames.

Tips

- Framing stores may give away scrap and excess materials.
- Some framing websites offer different size frames at overstock prices.
- Pictures purchased at garage sales can be replaced with children's work.
- Local shoe stores may donate shoe box lids.

Questions

- Is the signage grammatically correct?
- Are letters die-cut or computer generated?
- Have appropriate uppercase and lowercase letters been used?
- Are some signs child-made?
- Is there sufficient space between wall displays?
- Is the children's work displayed and grouped together by content?
- Does children's work display current learning experiences?
- Is most of the children's work framed with edges hidden, matted, or mounted?
- Is framed artwork placed at children's and adults' eye level?

organizing spaces into places of beauty

Spaces become more beautiful when they are organized. Display some items openly on shelves and place other collections in containers. Mix colorful children's toys with natural items to create a tranquil and inviting display.

A shelf filled with bins and baskets may keep things organized but isn't particularly inviting. With all the materials tucked away, children forget to explore the amazing items within. To encourage children to investigate, store items that are small and have many pieces in containers. Then, take some of these items out of their basket and display them next to or in front of the container. Making the items inside the container more visible encourages children to discover.

Teachers typically store classroom materials in brightly colored plastic baskets or bins. Although these baskets are functional, they are not aesthetically pleasing. Instead, consider using containers that are unique or reflect natural materials and colors.

Tips

- Incorporate neutral-colored bins, natural baskets, and/or transparent containers throughout the classroom.
- Organize shelves with a designated place for all materials.
- Create a system for children to use when retrieving and replacing objects (e.g., pictures/drawings and/or names of items on the shelf).
- Categorize objects and containers on each shelf with items that belong together (e.g., all the puzzles are on the same shelf).
- Allow blank spaces between objects on shelves.
- Find unique containers at garage sales and recycle shops.

Classifying materials is another way to create displays that enhance the environment. Children appreciate knowing their classroom items are stored in the same place from day to day. Children learn to value and respect classroom materials when you teach them to label, group, and store items in beautiful and systematic ways.

Ideas for unique storage

- vases
- wooden boxes
- muffin tins
- canisters
- tackle boxes
- metal tins
- flower pots
- sewing boxes
- cookie tins
- spice jars
- jewelry boxes
- empty paint cans
- acrylic tumblers
- wooden bowls
- lunch boxes
- acrylic water pitchers
- bushel baskets
- wooden barrels
- strawberry boxes
- office baskets
- plastic egg trays
- miniature suitcases
- hatboxes
- platters & trays
- metal pails
- ice buckets
- picnic baskets
- ice cube trays
- synthetic terra-cotta planters

raising storage displays to an artform

Many times, we store classroom materials in mundane containers because of convenience and necessity. A container to hold scissors, for example, can be an ordinary plastic bin—but with a little imagination, a brick becomes a practical and creative way of displaying these craft tools.

Store magnifying glasses in artificial grass.

Paintbrushes rest easily in corn kernels.

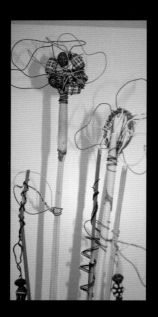

As summer came to an end, the children realized the leaves were beginning to fall off their favorite tree. They discussed what to give the tree so the tree would not be lonely when its leaves were gone. The children decided to make wire flowers because they were cheerful and would keep the tree company during the cold winter.

Maria, Pre-Kindergarten Teacher

principle 6: elements heighten ambiance

Sometimes a simple shadow from a window creates visual interest and draws you to an object or place.

-Sara Harris

Think of a special place where, from the moment you walk in, you know that you belong, feel comfortable, and want to return again and again. Why do you think you feel this way? Perhaps it is an emotional connection, a link to a childhood memory, or an attraction to the space's physical elements. It may be a place where you renew, revitalize, repair, or rejoice. Often, you may find its attraction originates with your body's senses of sight and sound.

shadow

glow

the element of light

Children explore the wondrous world of illumination as they manipulate the light and dark of shadows and silhouettes.

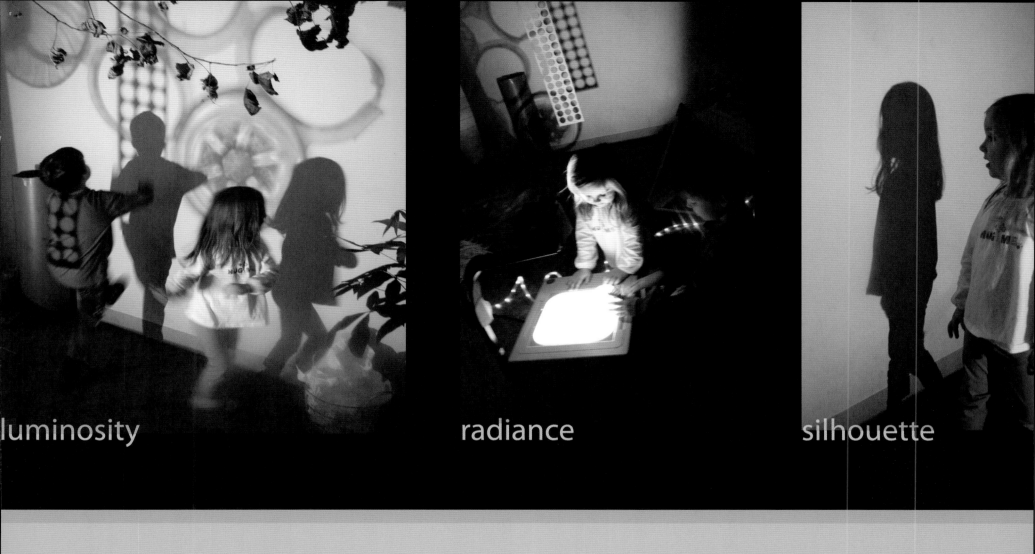

luminosity

radiance

silhouette

Light changes the way we perceive our environment.

To ensure maximum use of natural light, capture as much as you can. Be careful not to block incoming light with furniture or non-transparent materials. If possible, leave windows basically bare so children can see the outside world. Hang prisms or glass balls in front of the windows to create a beautiful space when sunlight dances and scatters color across the floor and ceiling.

illuminating spaces safely

Lighting sets the mood in any space, and it is especially true in an early chldhood classroom. A small chandelier can be adjusted with a dimmer. Other lights can intrigue children by stimulating them to create shadows and light patterns. With natural energy-efficient, and low-heat (e.g., LED) lighting, you can illuminate your classroom in an environmentally responsible way.

Tip

- Outdoor bulbs are inappropriate for a reading area because they are too bright and give off a cold, bluish hue. Look for safe, low-wattage, energy-efficient, and soft lighting for indoor spaces.

Ideas for shadow play props

- hats
- figurines
- costumes
- puppets
- plants
- nature items
- netting
- tissue paper
- jewels
- store-bought feathers
- transparent Items
- mirrors
- yarn
- twine
- recycled materials
- tubes
- textiles
- Plexiglas

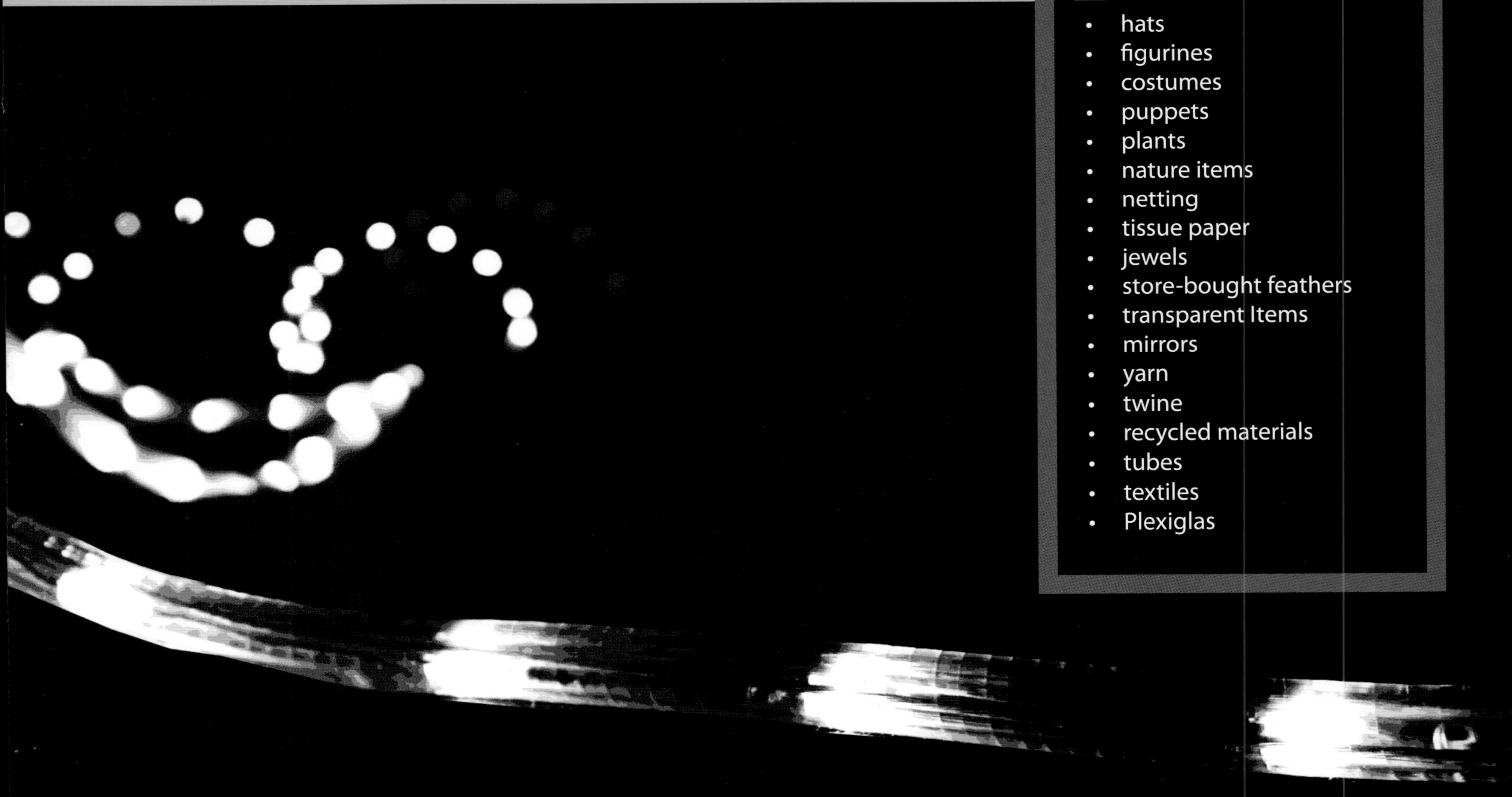

making spaces shine

Adding multiple light sources makes spaces shine, softens the area, and creates a positive ambiance. People who spend time in spaces with good lighting feel better about themselves and their work.

Ideas
for lighting

- spotlights
- recessed lights
- pole lamps
- chandeliers
- table lamps
- hanging lamps
- light boxes
- task lighting
- landscape lamps
- rope lights
- flashlights
- grow lights
- overhead projector
- dimmers
- three-way lights
- glow sticks
- pendant lights
- battery-powered lanterns
- torchieres
- octopus-style lights
- fiber optic lights
- sunlight
- battery-powered candles
- garden lights
- light tables
- sconces

Children create scenes of fantasy in a glowing underwater world by adding stones, clear beads, tree stumps, and plastic amphibians to a light table.

Illuminate your space to encourage children's interactions and dramatic experiences. Invite children to experiment with light tables and projectors. Encourage them to express their imaginations freely and explore the different qualities of light. They might discover that some materials work better on the light table while others make unique shadows as the light shines through them.

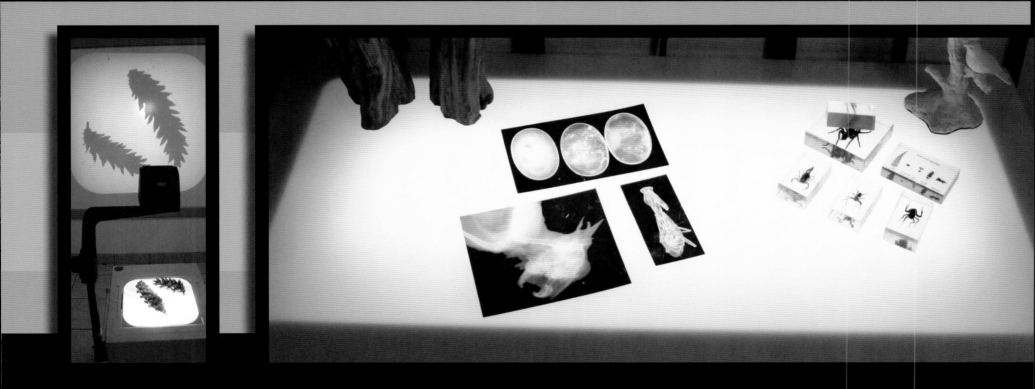

Dried oranges hang from a branch, creating a gorgeous, sunlit window.

creating sensory ambiance

Ambiance encompasses many senses. Soft lighting, soothing music, and the scent of freshly baked cookies create a home-like environment. Sounds, smells, textures, and lighting can evoke positive and negative responses. By recognizing the significant role your senses play in your attraction to an environment, you can construct your own space filled with enticing ambiance.

the element of sound

Be aware of how sounds affect children. The sound of a babbling brook, the gentle notes of a flute, or the breeze blowing across a wind chime all have a calming effect. Energetic band music, on the other hand, jumpstarts them and gets them moving. Compose various listening experiences to encourage children to explore their natural responses to the ambiance of sound.

Light
always follows the path of the
beautiful.

-Anonymous

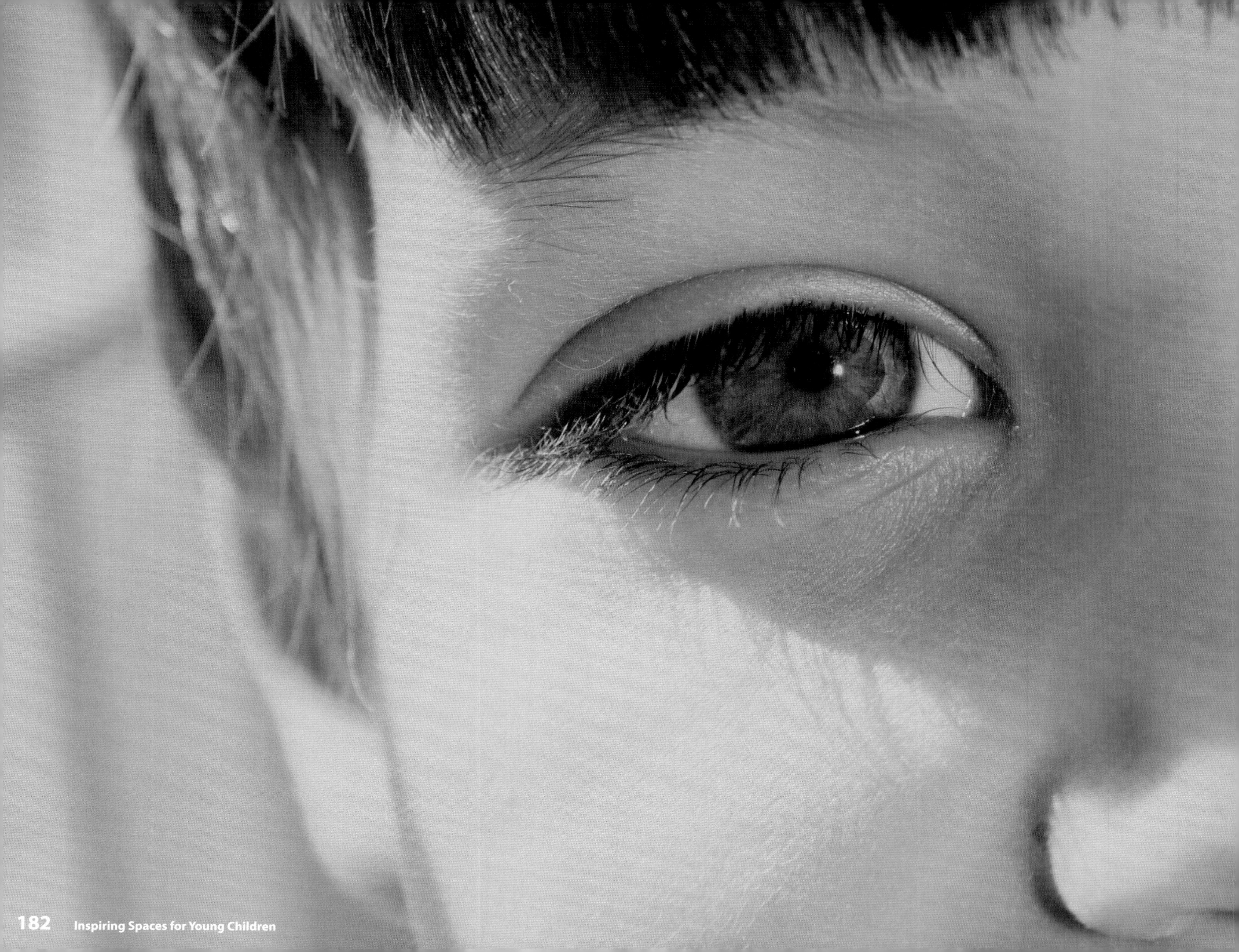

principle 7: focal points attract attention

A child can be drawn into a space by focal points created with architecture, furniture and its placement, and artwork.

-Sara Harris

Close your eyes for a moment . . .

Imagine walking into a place of worship. What is the first thing you envision in your mind's eye? Is it the praying bench, altar or pulpit, stained glass windows, organ, or statue? Ask a few people to participate in this experiment and to share with you the first thing that comes to their minds. They may visualize something quite different from you because of their perspectives, interests, values, and experiences. Some people, for example, may envision the organ or choir loft because music soothes their spirits and is emotionally relevant to them. Others may focus on the stained glass window because its beauty captures the essence of their personal worship. Regardless of what you envision when you close your eyes, it is safe to say that something popped into your mind's eye and that object is something you see immediately upon entering the sanctuary.

A classroom's focal point is similar to a sanctuary. When designing a focal point, it is important to think about the classroom's layout in relationship to children's interests, backgrounds, and experiences. An effective focal point draws children's eyes and entices them to explore the area's interesting elements. Also, a successful focal point forces the eyes to focus on the more important objects in the classroom instead of custodial components such as cubbies or coat racks.

Open your classroom door . . .

While standing at the door, bend down to view the space from the children's perspective. What do you see from this viewpoint? Do you see a focal point filled with custodial items such as cubbies or coat hooks? Or, were your eyes drawn to an interesting focal point that captured your attention? Effective focal points draw children to an area.

enhancing focal points

Focal points, which may be interactive or visual, can be enhanced through color, texture, and architectural elements. Areas where the walls have been visually enhanced give importance and draw attention to the space.

Tall, white walls are architecturally beautiful and exhibit a sense of openness. But when creating a space for children that is comfortable, inviting, and relaxing, those same large walls may seem vast and cold.

By visually enhancing the space to establish a focal point with textural table runners of calming colors, this cozy space is defined and children are embraced by its warmth.

Tips

When designing your focal points . . .

- Face shelves forward or perpendicular to the entry.
- Place all items to create a balance of empty and filled spaces on the walls.
- Incorporate interactive components that capture children's interest.
- Enhance your classroom with authentic, unique pieces, and extraordinary elements.
- Apply the Seven Principles of Design.

The focal point in this room is a wintry ice fishermen's scene. The wood beams represent a fishing shanty, and the secured clear blocks set the perimeter of the area. White cardboard blocks that the children can use to continue building the walls, a fishing hole made of wood with blue and stone patterned linoleum, a bench, and animals all add to the experience.

Most of us remember growing up making tents under our mom's kitchen table and chairs using the biggest blanket we could find. Our makeshift tent magically transformed us into adventurers who slept under the stars, ate from a tin can, and fought off grizzly bears.

Those wondrous times came to life once again for the children in my classroom with an authentic campsite. The camping area is filled with everything a child needs to go on an adventure—including a wall mural of a lake, trees, and birds that brings the glorious outdoors into the classroom.

Our children's faces light up when they begin cooking steaks and veggies on the grill, grab a backpack and go for a walk with their friends, or excitedly crawl into the sleeping bag to gaze up at the stars. Each camping experience is filled with many adventures and much excitement, rich and expressive language, and truly extraordinary moments.

-Sharon, Toddler Teacher

Ideas for authentic camping items

- sleeping bag
- charcoal grill
- cooler
- lantern
- pots and pans
- canteen
- backpack
- suitcase
- firewood
- artificial food
- log bench
- bale of hay
- tent
- tin coffee pot
- flashlight
- bug net
- fishing pole and fish
- hiking boots
- lawn chairs
- hammock
- binoculars
- camera

bringing children in

Focal points create an attractive, exciting place for children, especially when you approach the task with purpose. When you add an archway and bridge, or position equipment to create an entrance, the area becomes inviting and visually important. This well-defined space welcomes children and encourages them to explore simply through its design.

Tips

- Ask families to donate outdated road maps.
- Request city/town road signs no longer in use.
- Find someone with carpentry skills to construct a simple framework and anchor race cars.
- Add race car costumes.

These small pedal cars generate excitement as a focal point. The decoupaged maps and road signs add to the authentic experience.

When everything is emphasized,
nothing is emphasized.

-Aluer

Part

3

designing

The flourishing beauty of a blooming classroom is within your reach. You have gathered the seeds of knowledge about the important concepts found in the Seven Principles of Design. Nature, colors, furnishings, textures, displays, elements, and focal points all contribute to growing aesthetically pleasing spaces. Now it is time for you to apply this wealth of knowledge to cultivate inspiring spaces for young children.

prepping the soil

It does not matter if your classroom space is new, under renovation, or simply lacks aesthetic appeal, you need to first prep the soil before you implement the design. Maybe a teacher has mentioned that the classroom is looking worn. Perhaps an administrator has noticed that the excitement of the space is lacking. Or, an owner has the vision to remodel or build a new facility.

Regardless of where the spark begins, many people will be actively involved in the transformation of the space. Therefore, it is important to collaborate, identify each person's role, and determine who will be leading the project and fulfilling the group's vision.

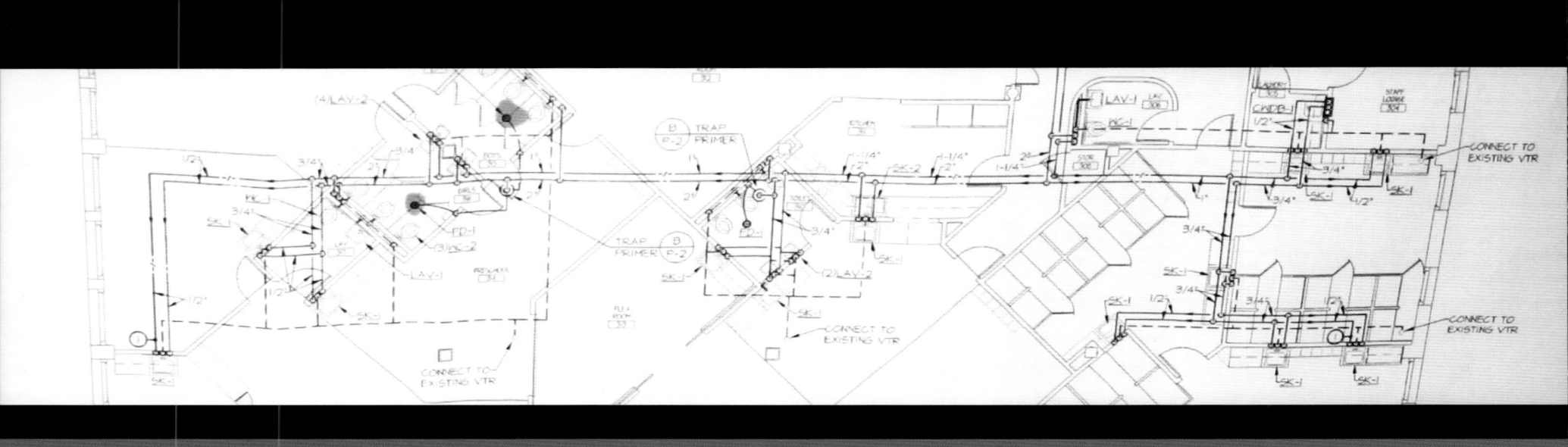

observing the ground

To begin viewing your space from a new perspective, think about a special place where you feel comfortable, energized, and welcomed. As you reflect on this space, you may realize that it has a powerful effect on you.

Now, observe your classroom objectively. This realistic viewpoint helps you understand what you need to do to grow your classroom into a blooming environment.

To guide you in objectively evaluating children's spaces, you can use the *Rating Observation Scale for Inspiring Environments* (ROSIE), which is available through Gryphon House, Inc. For more information, visit gryphonhouse.com.

determining soil conditions

Determine your current soil conditions by collaborating with teachers, administrators, designers, and children. To accurately measure the soil conditions, ask key questions. As you answer the questions on the following page you will identify the changes you wish to make and any key elements necessary to create a blooming space.

questions to consider

1. How many children will occupy the space?

2. What changes would make the most impact?

3. What changes would best enhance learning experiences?

4. Does the space accommodate the children's needs?

5. What materials are available for enhancing/renovating the room?

6. What purchases must be made to complete the vision for the room?

7. How can nature be brought into the space?

8. What is the project's budget?

9. How can the children's work personalize the space?

10. Which classroom area will become the focal point?

11. What are the space's constraints (i.e., window placement, classroom shape, architecture)?

12. Which features or areas should be highlighted?

13. If using the *Rating Observation Scale for Inspiring Environments* (ROSIE), what areas are Sprouting, Budding, or Blooming and why?

designing the landscape

1. Determine the room's size by measuring the length and height of walls, doors, and windows.

2. Consider the room's shape and architectural features when laying out your design.

3. Ensure all learning centers have been included in the design by checking them off as they are added to the layout. Circle areas on the graph that designate where centers should be located. When placing centers, consider their functions. For example, a quiet learning center should not be placed in the line of traffic or next to a loud area such as blocks. The science area may benefit from being close to windows or positioned on a hard flooring surface for sensory activities or scientific investigations. Also, remember to position your focal point so it is visible when entering the room.

4. Organize and keep each learning center's contents together. Items scattered throughout the classroom are visually confusing.

5. Define the learning centers on graph paper by drawing or placing cut-outs representing furniture. Be creative with the placement of shelves. Positioning furniture at 45-degree or 90-degree angles to walls creates separate and cozy spaces.

6. Create a list of smaller items needed for enhancing each learning center. Think about how the walls, ceiling, floor, shelves, and tables complete the overall look of each area.

7. Find ways to stimulate children's excitement by encouraging them to give their work as gifts to the room. Not only do these gifts personalize the classroom, but they honor children's work.

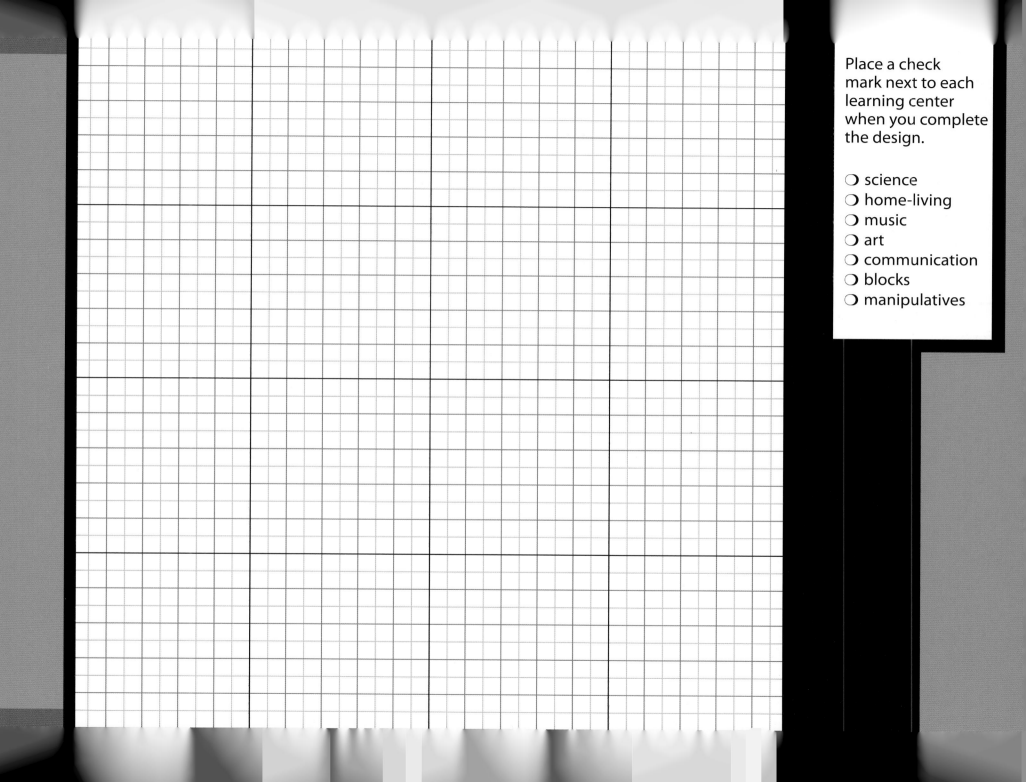

Place a check mark next to each learning center when you complete the design.

○ science
○ home-living
○ music
○ art
○ communication
○ blocks
○ manipulatives

selecting inspirational elements

Many people do not know what they like until they see it. Create an idea notebook, design board, or inspiration file to bring together potential classroom components. Whether you manually cut and paste images from magazines or create a virtual design board by dragging images from websites, these processes help to visualize the aesthetic appeal of the total composition.

A picture, branch, rug, or curtain may inspire a color scheme, style, and focal point. Many times, inspiration comes from designer or authentic pieces that can be re-created or altered. For example, adjusting the height of adult furniture by shortening the legs makes the size appropriate for young children.

You can establish a color scheme by choosing a favorite furnishing element. If this inspirational piece has many colors, select one color that coordinates with your existing pieces. When used sparingly, a pop of color generates interest. A complementary or coordinating color may also be integrated into the space. Be careful not to create visual chaos by overloading your classroom color palette.

revealing your design

After you have collaborated with your team, drawn a layout, and selected an inspiration piece, it is time to share your vision with everyone involved. When revealing the design, try to be open to comments and suggestions that may lead to beneficial adjustments in the plan.

Looking at the design plan on paper helps to envision the layout, but walking around the room with the design in hand encourages everyone to determine the layout's practicality and feasibility. Ask your team to imagine what it would be like to be a child exploring and learning in each area. Ask if the design will work or if you need to make changes.

After the team views the space, determine necessary adjustments. Keeping the budget in mind, apply these changes to the design plan. Finally, reiterate what is needed to complete the project, and be sure everyone knows their roles for implementation.

preparing for planting

Just as you would not begin planting a garden with only half of your supplies, you need to gather the needed resources for your design plan before you begin. Once you have all the necessary items, schedule a time to begin executing the room design.

Remove wall decor before work begins, spackle, and paint so the room is fresh and ready for its makeover. Arrange for people with the necessary carpentry and mechanical skills to assist. See Principle 2, Color Generates Interest, for tips on choosing paint colors.

planting and growing your garden

Design Layout

Blank Canvas

We suggest that no more than five and no fewer than three people help with the classroom design. The lead person should organize each participant's role in the set-up. Make sure the room's new layout is available so each person knows where items belong.

Start with a blank canvas. Complete any painting or repairs before set-up.

Before

Classroom A

Large Furniture

Final Layout

First, position the large furniture. To keep everyone actively participating in the set-up phase, stronger people might move shelving while others can move toys or wall hangings.

After the larger furniture is in place, begin layering the space with many different textiles and finishes. Rugs, wall art, shelves, lighting, mobiles, and hooks are important in creating the finished product.

Organize existing materials in shelves, bins, and cupboards. Display these items in natural baskets, bins in similar colors or materials, and on open shelves to magnetize children's attention.

Position any items you have purchased or made to reflect the new color scheme. These items add interest and visual energy and invite children to view the entire space.

making spaces bloom

Bland and cluttered spaces are uninspiring. Now it is time to turn this space into a blooming place.

The "Before" photo shows that the classroom teacher has tried to beautify the space. However, seeing the back of the shelf, worn upholstered chairs, disproportionate pillow to chair and chairs to table sizes, and out-of-place artwork make this space appear uninspiring.

Before

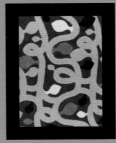

Child-made Artwork   Soft Lighting   Authentic Furnishings   Rug

This new and blooming space boasts soft lighting, child-made artwork, authentic furnishings, plants, and rugs.

Design Layout

Blank Canvas

Before

Classroom B

Large Furniture

Final Layout

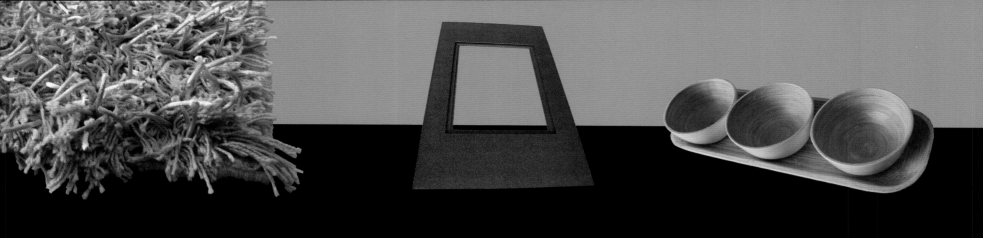

Children are curious. They want to touch everything and learn by doing. Responding to their natural interest in texture, we created a texture board. Rugs, plastic grass, smooth acrylic mirrors, wooden place mats, bumpy matting frames, and seagrass wallpaper stimulate children's senses. The children can crawl across the board, sit and touch the many textures, and even add their own textural items to the wooden bowls and fabric-lined trays provided in the area.

personalizing space

Even with beautiful layouts and room designs, classrooms can lack children's personalities. There are many ways to visually reflect the lives of the children throughout the room, such as encouraging them to give their creations as gifts to the classroom.

ABCDEF
GHIJKL
MNOPQR
STUVWX
YZ

Nature is not only beautiful, calming, and inspiring, but it can also be a teacher . . . a cause for reaction . . . an interactive tool for cognitive development. Whether children are categorizing sticks by length, rocks by weight, and shells by color, they are developing many problem-solving skills that they can use throughout their lives. Allowing yourself and the children to see natural objects as items that can be manipulated and sorted in many ways can take manipulative play beyond sorting plastic pieces at a table to limitless learning anywhere.

Children infuse their own personality and interests into a room by giving gifts they have created to various areas. The children who created the scene below were interested in animals and their habitats. After visiting a local zoo, the children decided to create their own zoo for their play animals. They gathered small boxes and drew images on them to identify the types of buildings each box represent. Through this activity, the children created items that reflected their interests and extended dramatic play into their block area.

Encouraging children's interactions with nature offers many benefits. A little seed in a child's hand can evoke questions, "What can this little seed become?" "What does it need to grow?" "How tall can it get?" Giving children the responsibility of taking care of a little seedling gives them purpose and worth. Measuring that little plant as it grows helps children to learn about size, comparisons, and numbers. The children may decide to measure it in various ways . . . with their hands, a ruler, a tape measure, or leaves. They become a part of the process as they grow and learn.

Giving children open-ended, natural materials and a blank space in which to create provides a unique environment with limitless possibilities. The space transforms into an original work of art as the children interact in this area every day.

Steps to make a rock sculpture center

- Base is cut into a 4'x4' piece of plywood.
- Landscape pavers outline and define sculpture area.
- Planter boxes filled with different colored rocks add spatial boundaries and make children's building materials readily available.

Re-evaluating your garden design

From the first step into the classroom, it is important that both children and adults feel inspired and welcome. Although you have made intentional choices about the furnishings, definition of centers, personalization of space, and organization of learning materials—something still may be lacking. It is important to allow yourself time to re-evaluate what you have created.

By looking at the space again, you may develop a new list of things that need to be tweaked, added, or even removed. Make a list of the changes you think are needed and determine when and by whom they should be done. Giving yourself permission to make changes to your well-developed and thoughtful plan can ultimately help you reach your final goal of a blooming environment.

When all is complete, take the opportunity to look around the room at the beauty you have created. Appreciate all that you have done to turn this children's space into a blooming garden of aesthetic appeal. And, although you have worked hard to grow this flourishing space, do not forget that even a beautiful garden can die without water. Revisit the space every few months to ensure that the splendor continues to grow.

items still needed to complete the design

1. _____

2. _____

3. _____

4. _____

5. _____

6. _____

7. _____

8. _____

9. _____

10. _____

Index

Resources

Gas Pumps

www.thefinestwebsiteforgaspumps.com

www.oldtymegaspumps.com

Pedal Cars

www.RidingToys.com/PedalCars

www.Kotulas.com/Toys

www.BuyElectricScooter.com/Pedal-Cars

www.amazon.com

Race Car Costumes

www.CostumeSuperCenter.com

www.nextag.com

www.target.com

Store Mannequins

www.mannequinstore.com

Street Signs

www.trafficsignstore.com

www.usa_traffic_signs.com

www.ricesigns.com

www.Mr.StreetSigns.com

www.signssupercheap.com

www.roadsigncollection.com

Table Runners

www.williams-sonoma.com

www.TableRunner.Pronto.com

www.pier1.com

www.novica.com   (natural fibers)

www.target.com

Additional Website Resources

Classroom Cool
http://www.nea.org/neatoday/0504/classroomcool.html

Aesthetics in the Classroom
http://www.ccie.com/eed/issue.php?id=1996

An Introduction to Learning and Teaching (excerpt p. 117-149)
http://books.google.com/books?id=eOEwMmNt9ygC&pg=PA117&lpg=PA117&dq=aest
hetics+%2Bclassroom&source=web&ots=37DX37I9-G&sig=eNNyIJvuHCHIVF0YRhkUIIA
hFQU&hl=en&sa=X&oi=book_result&resnum=10&ct=result#PPA117,M1

Classroom Food for Thought (list of links)
http://www.classroom.umn.edu/foodforthought.asp

K-12 Classroom Design: Remarkable Learning Places (abstract, looks useful/interesting)
http://www.asid.org/events/ceus/pocket/pocketclemons1.htm

Aesthetics and Ethics in Everyday Life (?)
http://www.goshen.edu/art/ed/housetor.html

The 100 is There!   (Reggio)
http://www.designshare.com/index.php/articles/hundred-1

http://www.communityplaythings.com/resources/articles/designingenvironments/
index.html

Tips of the Trade: 8 Ways to Make Classroom Really Inspiring http://www.teachernet.gov.
uk/teachers/issue33/secondary/features/Classrooms_Secondary/

Reggio Emilia Approach
http://www.brainy-child.com/article/reggioemilia.html

http://www.nea.org/classmanagement/rh050324.html
Feng shui – soft edges, rounded corners

Aesthetics in the Classroom
http://www.ccie.com/eed/issue.php?id=1996

Consider the Walls
http://journal.naeyc.org/btj/200405/walls.asp

Aesthetic Codes in Early Childhood Classrooms (Reggio)
http://www.designshare.com/Research/Tarr/Aesthetic_Codes_1.htm

Plants in the Classroom
http://www.usask.ca/education/coursework/mcvittiej/resources/livingthings/plants.
htm

A New Beginning (organizing a classroom)
http://www.teachingk-8.com/archives/your_first_year/a_new_beginning_by_peter_w_
cookson_jr.html

Defining Elements in the Planning of Early Childhood Classrooms
http://www.eric.ed.gov/ERICDocs/data/ericdocs2sql/content_
storage_01/0000019b/80/16/02/29.pdf

Psychological Properties of Colours
http://www.colour-affects.co.uk/psyprop.html

Landscape for Learning: The Impact of Classroom Design on Infants and Toddlers
http://www.earlychildhoodnews.com/earlychildhood/article_view.aspx?ArticleID=238

Power of Aesthetics to Improve Student Learning
http://www.designshare.com/index.php/articles/aesthetics-and-learning/

Essential Criteria for an Ideal Learning Environment
http://www.newhorizons.org/strategies/learning_environments/lang.htm

Reinventing Learning Spaces
http://www.newhorizons.org/strategies/learning_environments/hunkins.html

Environments for Learning
http://www.newhorizons.org/strategies/learning_environments/front_lrnenvironments.
htm

The Optimal Learning Environment: Learning Theories
http://www.designshare.com/index.php/articles/the-optimal-learning-environment-
learning-theories/

Design of Child Care Centers and Effects of Noise on Young Children
http://www.designshare.com/index.php/articles/chronic-noise-and-children/

Brain-based Learning, Optimal Environments
http://www.isu.edu/ctl/nutshells/old_nutshells/8_8.htm

Learning, Lighting and Color
http://www.designshare.com/articles/1/133/fielding_light-learn-color.pdf

References

Aluer, D. (1990). Design basics. Orlando, FL: Harcourt Brace Jovanovich.

Ceppi, G., & Zini, M. (Eds.). (1998). Children, spaces, relations: Meta-project for an environment for young children. Reggio Emilia, Italy: Reggio Children.

Carter, D., & Carter, M. (2003). Designs for living and learning: Transforming early childhood environments. St. Paul, MN: Redleaf Press.

Copple, C., & Bredekamp, S. (Eds.). (2009). Developmentally appropriate practice in early childhood programs serving children from birth through age 8 (3rd ed.). Washington, DC: NAEYC.

Duncan, S. (2009). Bringing beauty and nature home. Plymouth, NH: Megaprint.

Edwards, C., Gandini, L., & Forman, G. (1998). The hundred languages of children: The Reggio Emilia approach—Advanced reflections (2nd ed.). Greenwich, CT: Ablex.

Fraser, S., & Gestwicki, C. (2002). Authentic childhood: Exploring Reggio Emilia in the classroom. Clifton Park, NY: Thomson Delmar Learning.

Frost, J. (2010). A history of children's play and play environments. New York: Routledge Press.

Gandini, L., Hill, L., Cadwell, L., & Schwall, C. (Eds.). (2005). In the spirit of the studio: Learning from the atelier of Reggio Emilia. New York, NY: Teachers College Press.

Gardner, H. (2006). Multiple intelligences: New horizons. New York, NY: Basic Books.

Gardner, H. (2006). Five minds for the future. Boston, MA: Harvard Business School Press.

Greenman, J. (1988). Caring spaces, learning places: Children's environments that work. Redmond, WA: Exchange Press.

Greenman, J. (1987, November). Thinking about the aesthetics of children's environments. Child Care Information Exchange, 58, 9-12.

Harms, T., Clifford, R., & Cryer, D. (1998). Early childhood environment rating scale (Rev. ed.). New York: Teachers College Press.

Hertzog, N. (2001). Reflections and impressions from Reggio Emilia: "It's not about art!" Early Childhood Research and Practice, 3(1). On-line at: http://ecrp.uluc.edu/v3n/hertzog.html.

Humphryes, J. (2000, March). Exploring nature with children. Young Children, 55(2), 16-20.

Isbel, R., & Exelby, B. (2001). Early learning environments that work. Beltsville, MD: Gryphon House.

Keeler, R. (2008). Natural playscapes: Creating outdoor play environments for the soul. Redmond, WA: Exchange Press.

Kellert, S., & Kahn, P. (2002). Children and nature. Cambridge, MA: MIT Press.

Kempton, W., Boster, J., & Hartley, J. (1995). Environmental values in American culture. Cambridge, MA: MIT Press.

Lemmon, J. (2004). Putting the heart in your home. Des Moines, IA: Meredith Corporation.

LeVan, M. (2002). Nature Style: Elegant decorating with leaves, twigs & stones. New York, NY: Lark Books.

Lewin-Benham, A. (2008). Powerful children: Understanding how to teach and learn using the Reggio approach. New York: Teachers College Press, 2008.

Louv, R. (2005). Last child in the woods: Saving our children from nature-deficit disorder. Chapel Hill, NC: Algonquin Books of Chapel Hill.

Lynch, S. (2003). 77 habits of highly creative interior designers. Glouchester, MA: Rockport Publishers.

Parikh, A. (1994). Making the most of small spaces. New York, NY: Rizzoli International Publications, Inc.

Rui-Olds, A. (2001). Child care design guide. New York, NY: McGraw Hill.

Smith, L. (2005). Discovering home: Find your personal style. Des Moines, IA: Meredith Books.

Sobel, D. (2008). Childhood and nature: Design principles for educators. Portland, WA: Stenhouse Publishers.

Stirling, S. (2006). Babyspace idea book. Newton, CT: Taunton Home.

Tarr, P. (2003). Reflections on the image of the child reproducer or creator of culture. Art Education, 56(4), 6-11.

Tarr, P. (2004, May). Consider the Walls. Young Children, (57)3, 33-41.

Wurm, J. (2005). Working in the Reggio way: A beginner's guide for American teachers. St. Paul, MN: Redleaf Press.